ENGINEERING
DISASTERS

AIR FRANCE FLIGHT 447

BY TODD KORTEMEIER

CONTENT CONSULTANT
Lance Sherry, PhD; Director, Center for Air Transportation Systems Research; George Mason University

Cover image: Workers pulled the tail of Flight 447 out of the ocean on June 14, 2009.

Core Library
An Imprint of Abdo Publishing
abdobooks.com

abdobooks.com

Published by Abdo Publishing, a division of ABDO, PO Box 398166, Minneapolis, Minnesota 55439.

Printed in the United States of America, North Mankato, Minnesota
092019
012020

THIS BOOK CONTAINS RECYCLED MATERIALS

Cover Photo: Evaristo SA/AFP/Getty Images
Interior Photos: Evaristo SA/AFP/Getty Images, 1; Eliyahu Yosef Parypa/Shutterstock Images, 4–5; Jaromir Chalabala/Shutterstock Images, 8; Walbe/Correio do Estado/AP Images, 10; Shutterstock Images, 12–13, 43; Angelo Giampiccolo/Shutterstock Images, 15; Red Line Editorial, 17; Brazilian Air Force/dapd/AP Images, 18; Eraldo Peres/AP Images, 20–21; Roberto Candia/AP Images, 23; Fred Scheiber/AP Images, 25; Christophe Ena/AP Images, 28–29; Michel Euler/AP Images, 30, 45; Golden Sikorka/Shutterstock Images, 32; Victor R. Caivano/AP Images, 36–37; Carlos E. Santa Maria/Shutterstock Images, 39

Editor: Marie Pearson
Series Designer: Ryan Gale

Library of Congress Control Number: 2019941995

Publisher's Cataloging-in-Publication Data

Names: Kortemeier, Todd, author.
Title: Air France flight 447 / by Todd Kortemeier
Description: Minneapolis, Minnesota : Abdo Publishing, 2020 | Series: Engineering disasters | Includes online resources and index.
Identifiers: ISBN 9781532190704 (lib. bdg.) | ISBN 9781532176555 (ebook)
Subjects: LCSH: Air France Flight 447 Crash, 2009--Juvenile literature. | Disasters--Juvenile literature. | Engineering--Juvenile literature. | Airbus A330 (Jet transport)--Juvenile literature. | Aircraft accidents--Juvenile literature.
Classification: DDC 363.12465--dc23

CONTENTS

CHAPTER ONE

A HUGE STORM

It was the early morning of June 1, 2009. For the passengers and crew of Air France Flight 447, all seemed normal cruising over the Atlantic Ocean. Three hours earlier, the Airbus A330 had taken off from Rio de Janeiro, Brazil. Its passengers were a mix of vacationers and business travelers. The flight was due for an 11:10 a.m. arrival in Paris, France.

The aircraft reached its cruising altitude of 35,000 feet (11,000 m). Captain Marc Dubois took a break. Pilots are allowed to work for only so many hours in a row. Dubois's break ensured he could be back at the controls in the cockpit when the aircraft landed.

Air France Flight 447 was flown with an A330.

Copilots David Robert and Pierre-Cedric Bonin took over the controls.

Shortly after the captain left, Robert and Bonin looked at the weather map on the computer screen. It showed a giant storm ahead of them. The storm was too big to fly around or over. They were going to have to fly through it, avoiding the worst part of the storm. It was going to be a bumpy ride. They turned on the seat belt sign.

THE A330

The Airbus A330 had a long history by the time of the crash. It first flew in November 1992. As of 2019, the aircraft was still in production. The specific aircraft that flew Flight 447 was an A330-200 model. It was still relatively new at the time of the crash. It had been delivered to the airline in April 2005. It had been in a ground collision in 2006. Otherwise it had no accidents. In April 2009, worn parts had been replaced.

ICY CONDITIONS

Lightning lit up the night sky. The cold, humid air started to form ice on the aircraft. Ice can be dangerous to aircraft. It changes the shape of the smooth, curved wings. This makes the plane hard to control. Ice can also freeze up the plane's sensors. It makes them give false airspeed and altitude readings. The pilots turned on the heaters built into the sensors to melt the ice.

Suddenly, the three airspeed indicators gave different readings. The pilots had no idea how fast the plane was really going. Then an alarm sounded. The autopilot had turned itself off. The autopilot flies the aircraft. Without it, the pilots were forced to fly the plane manually.

Alarms buzzed and lights flashed in the cockpit. It was hard to think. Bonin thought there may be calmer air above the clouds. He pulled back on the joystick. The aircraft began to climb. He forgot that the autopilot was turned off. It would not keep him from steering the aircraft too fast or too slow. Airplanes fly when the air flows smoothly over the curved wings from front to back. The faster the air flows the better. When the air

Ice can be dangerous for airplanes, but there are systems to remove ice before and during flights.

flow is too slow, the airplane goes into an aerodynamic stall. It begins to fall out of the sky.

Shortly after Bonin nosed the aircraft up, a stall warning sounded. This alerted the pilots the plane was going too slowly. The pilots needed to point the nose of the aircraft down and descend. This would let the air flow over the wings again. The plane would resume flying.

THE CRASH

Captain Dubois could feel that something was not right. He rushed back to the cockpit. It was a confusing scene. He asked the copilots what they were doing.

The plane was dropping quickly. But the nose of the plane was up with the engines at full power. Dubois quickly told Bonin and Robert to push the nose down and gain speed. The plane started to recover. But by then they

PERSPECTIVES

FORCES FOR GOOD LOST

Among the lives lost on Flight 447 were Pablo Dreyfus and Ronald Dreyer. Both men were activists in Brazil. They sought to stop the trade of illegal firearms and drugs. Both had worked with the Brazilian government for years to try to stop these illegal activities. The men were on their way to Geneva, Switzerland. They were due to present a handbook on how to stop the sale of illegal weapons. Dreyfus had lived in Rio de Janeiro since 2002 with his wife, Ana Carolina Rodrigues, who was also on board Flight 447.

BRASIL
CGU-1/B

were only approximately 2,000 feet (600 m) above the water. It was too late. The plane slammed into the Atlantic Ocean. It broke up on impact.

All 228 passengers and crew died. No distress call was ever received. Nobody even knew the plane was missing at first. When dawn broke, the whole world would be wondering what happened to Air France Flight 447.

EXPLORE ONLINE

Chapter One describes what a stall is and how it can be dangerous to airplanes. Explore the website below and compare and contrast that information with this chapter. How does the website support this chapter? Did you learn anything new?

WHY DO AIRPLANES STALL AND WHY IS IT SO DANGEROUS?

abdocorelibrary.com/air-france-flight-447

Members of the Brazilian armed forces were some of the first to search for Flight 447.

CHAPTER **TWO**

THE SEARCH

Air France operated Flight 447 daily between Rio and Paris. Approximately one-half of the passengers were French or Brazilian. But people from 30 other countries were on board too.

An Airbus A330 only needs two pilots to fly. But this flight had three. The flight was longer than a pilot is allowed to work. There were pilots to take over when one took a break.

Captain Dubois was an experienced pilot. He had flown nearly 11,000 hours. He had been with the airline for more than 20 years. He was 58 but had no plans to retire.

Flight 447 took off from the Rio de Janeiro-Galeão International Airport.

Copilot Robert, 37, had been with Air France since 1998. He had more than 6,500 hours in the air. Copilot Bonin was the youngest at 32. He had been with Air France since 2003. He was approaching 3,000 hours in the air.

A NORMAL FLIGHT

Flight 447 took off at 7:30 p.m. local time. On board the aircraft, it was 10:30 p.m. Planes fly across many different places and time zones. So aircraft use Coordinated Universal Time (UTC) to determine a single time to use on board.

The plane's flight path took it along Brazil's coast. Then it turned to head across the Atlantic Ocean. At 1:35 a.m. UTC, the aircraft was 350 miles (565 km) off the northeastern coast of Brazil. The pilots reported they were cruising at 35,000 feet (11,000 m). All was normal. That was the last radio communication received. The aircraft then dropped off radar at 1:49 a.m. That alone was not unusual. Radar tracking stations are

Radar is useful in keeping track of airplane locations. But some areas in the ocean are not covered by radar.

on land. They can only track aircraft for a limited distance off the coast.

THE SEARCH BEGINS

When Flight 447 failed to reappear on radar, a lightning strike was suspected. But that was unlikely to knock a

FLIGHT 445

Air France changed the flight number of the route shortly after the crash. It operated as Flight 445 in November 2009 when an eerily similar incident occurred. The aircraft, also an Airbus A330-200, encountered turbulence near the same spot where Flight 447 disappeared. The turbulence lasted for approximately 30 minutes, while the crew descended to avoid it. The flight then continued as normal.

plane out of the sky. Planes are frequently struck by lightning with no problems.

The plane was due to pass through Senegal's airspace in West Africa. Planes from Senegal were the first sent out to find the missing Airbus. More planes from Brazil and the United States joined them. With only the plane's last known location to go on, the search began over a massive area of ocean. By the next day, a few traces of the plane were found. Two debris fields were spotted 220 miles (355 km) off the northeastern coast of Brazil. One was 3 miles (5 km) long. But it contained just a few scattered parts, such as an airplane seat and pieces

THE SEARCH AREA

Flight 447 was nearly in the middle of the Atlantic Ocean when it disappeared. That left few clues for where the search team should start to look. It took days before any significant trace of the plane was discovered. How do you think search crews picked a place to start looking?

When the tail was found largely intact, some speculated the airliner had broken apart before hitting the water.

of metal. There were no survivors to be found. In terms of loss of life, Flight 447 was the worst accident in the history of Air France. It was also the deadliest crash of any aircraft since November 2001.

The search continued for days. The first bodies were recovered June 6. On June 8, the aircraft's tail fin was hauled out of the ocean. Still missing were the aircraft's cockpit voice recorder (CVR) and flight data recorder (FDR). These are commonly known as the black boxes. The CVR records the pilots' conversations.

The FDR tracks the movements a plane makes, its speed, altitude, and more. The two boxes are durable enough to survive crashes and help investigators find out what went wrong.

Until the CVR and FDR were found, investigators could only guess what happened to Flight 447. The debris helped fill in some of the blanks. But it would take years to fill in the rest.

PERSPECTIVES

REMEMBERING THE VICTIMS

Anne and Michael Harris lived an adventurous life. The American couple were traveling on Flight 447 to attend a seminar in Paris. They also planned to work in some vacation time. Their friends and family remembered them as people who "loved life." Their niece described them: "Definitely glass-half-full kind of people," she said. "I think the initial shock of it all has really started to wear off, and the reality that they're gone is starting to set in. . . . The grief and the grieving process is beginning and we're just really focused on helping each other heal."

CHAPTER
THREE

THE INVESTIGATION

The search for Flight 447 continued for weeks. By June 26, more than 120,000 square miles (320,000 sq km) had been searched. The effort involved 1,100 members of the Brazilian navy. Investigators were left to comb through the 640 pieces of debris that had been pulled from the water.

The debris gave a few clues. Based on the damage, investigators could tell the plane did not break up in flight. All the destruction happened when the plane struck the water. They also could tell the plane was flying level.

Search crews brought the bodies they could find back home.

It was not diving. Life jackets had not been used, so passengers did not know they were about to crash.

DUAL INVESTIGATIONS

The Flight 447 investigation happened on two fronts. First there was the technical investigation. This looked at the cause of the crash. This investigation included investigators from many nations, including the United States' National Transportation Safety Board. There was also a criminal investigation. This investigation aimed to find out if Air France was legally responsible for the deaths of the passengers. The investigation took place in the French criminal justice system. Ten years after the disaster, the case had yet to go to trial.

A PUZZLE

It was a strange set of circumstances. How could a plane, flying level, be crashing with none of the passengers knowing? A clue came from the plane's automated messages. These are messages aircraft send to the ground when there is a problem.

In the minutes before the crash,

Investigators studied pieces of the wreckage to try to figure out how the accident had happened.

> **PERSPECTIVES**
>
> ## AN INVESTIGATOR
>
> Greg Feith is an investigator with the National Transportation Safety Board. He has participated in thousands of investigations. He did not work on the Flight 447 case. But he was alarmed at how French investigators expressed their doubts early on that the CVR and FDR would be found. He said, "Even if they are never found or the wreckage is never fully uncovered, they shouldn't give up this early—not only from an accident investigation standpoint, but also from the perspective of the families."

Flight 447 sent out many messages. One had to do with airspeed. The readings of the plane's instruments were unclear. They either weren't working or displayed conflicting speed readings. It was difficult for the flight crew to tell how fast the plane was going.

This was particularly important in bad weather and at night when pilots cannot see the horizon. Flight 447 had been flying into a thunderstorm. Heavy winds and freezing rain can

The pitot tube used on the Airbus 330

affect a plane's ability to fly. Knowing the plane's speed is essential to keep it from stalling.

AN EQUIPMENT PROBLEM?

The storm was not severe enough to cause major problems. A jet should have been able to easily fly through it. The nature of the problem pointed investigators to the aircraft's pitot tubes. Pitot tubes are located on the front of the plane. Air flows into the tubes. The tubes use the airspeed to measure how fast the airplane is going. If ice had clogged up the pitot tubes, then that could have caused the confusing speed readings.

The problem with pitot tubes was nothing new. In fact, Airbus had recommended to airlines in 2008 that the pitot tubes be replaced with improved models. In the aftermath of Flight 447, airlines began replacing them later that summer.

The pitot tubes seemed like they were a factor in the crash. But investigators were still just guessing. Without the CVR and FDR, they had very little evidence. The search for passengers ended, but the search for the CVR and FDR continued.

They were not going to be easy to find. In the middle of the Atlantic Ocean, they were more than 10,000 feet (3,000 m) deep. Black boxes had never been found at such a depth before. They send out signals of their location. But the signals only last for 30 days. Investigators admitted that it was possible the black boxes would never be found.

STRAIGHT TO THE SOURCE

In 2018, an anonymous former Air France Boeing 777 captain explained how a lack of training led to the confusion on Flight 447 when the sensors failed:

> *Training on speed failure in a simulator was very rare and during my 25 years practice on French airlines—before 2009—I must have been trained maximum 3 times in a simulator for this situation [speed sensor failure], while we were having at least 2 engine failures to deal with at every simulator session.*
>
> *I do not know why speed failure was not trained. This kind of failure can be very stressing. . . . In the early years of the A320 we still had an incidence-meter (angle of attack meter, not installed on the A330) but still it is not easy and to rely on instruments, when real and false alarms are raised together.*

Source: Tom Dieusaert. "Would Air France F447 Have Happened with Boeing?" *AeroTime*. AeroTime, June 1, 2018. Web. Accessed July 18, 2019.

Back It Up

The B777 pilot is using evidence to support a point. Write a paragraph describing the point the pilot is making. Then write down two or three pieces of evidence the pilot uses to make the point.

CHAPTER
FOUR

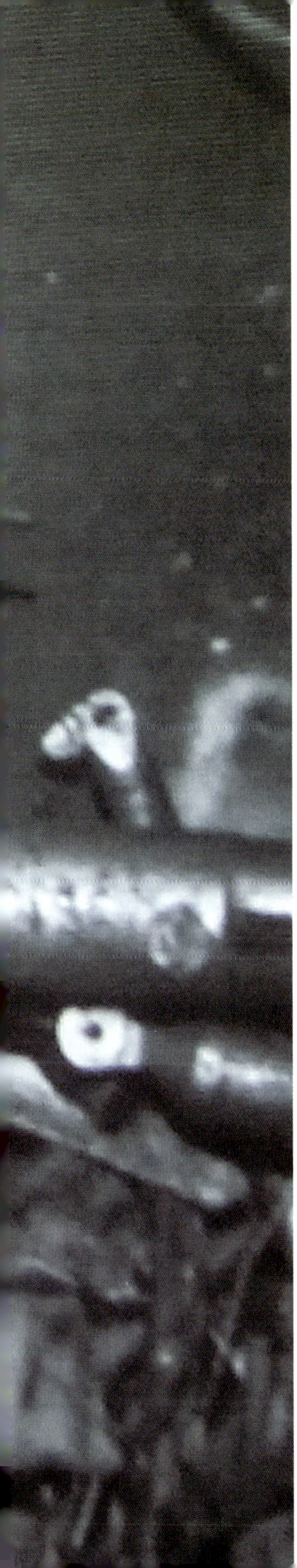

THE BLACK BOXES SPEAK

The search for Flight 447's CVR and FDR lasted nearly two years. It cost $30 million. And it took a little bit of luck. The wreckage was in even deeper water than previously thought. In April 2011, the plane's debris field was discovered in more than 13,000 feet (4,000 m) of water 600 miles (1,000 km) off the coast of Brazil. It was only approximately 6 miles (10 km) away from Flight 447's last known location on radar. A group of statistics experts used ocean currents and previous failed searches to predict where the wreckage would be.

Pictures of Flight 447's wreckage were released to the press in April 2011.

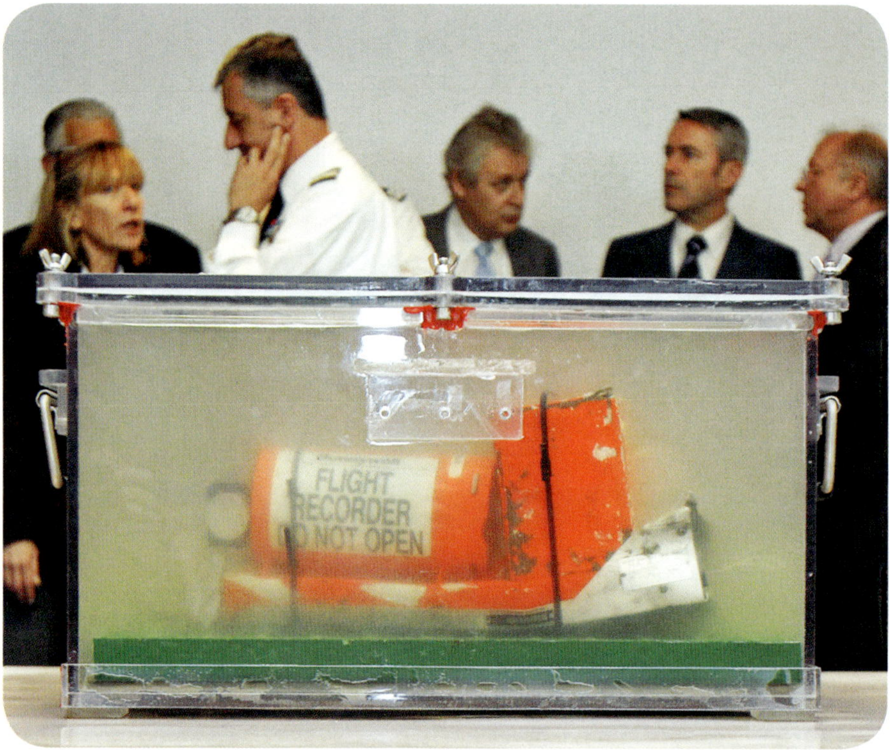

The black boxes held the flight records, including all the moves the copilots made just before the crash.

Once the wreckage was located, finding the black boxes was the top priority. The researchers also discovered more than 50 bodies of passengers.

HEARING THE PILOTS

The two black boxes were in good condition considering how long they had been underwater. But investigators did not know whether they still held any data. Fortunately, all the data was intact. And it painted a detailed picture of just what happened to Flight 447.

As suspected, ice jammed the pitot tubes. This caused an incorrect airspeed reading. The autopilot system disengaged. The crew took manual control of the plane. The plane was still fully functional. But the crew did not have all the flight information they normally would.

The conflicting sensor information made things confusing. It was hard to know what was happening. Without all the information, the copilots made some errors. Bonin pulled back on the stick. The aircraft began to climb. This action caused it to lose speed. A warning sounded to let the pilots know the plane was in a stall. But they ignored the alarm.

Suddenly, a pitot tube cleared. The crew could see how slowly they were flying. The pilots pushed the stick down. The plane was still climbing, but not as steeply.

CVR AND FDR LOCATIONS

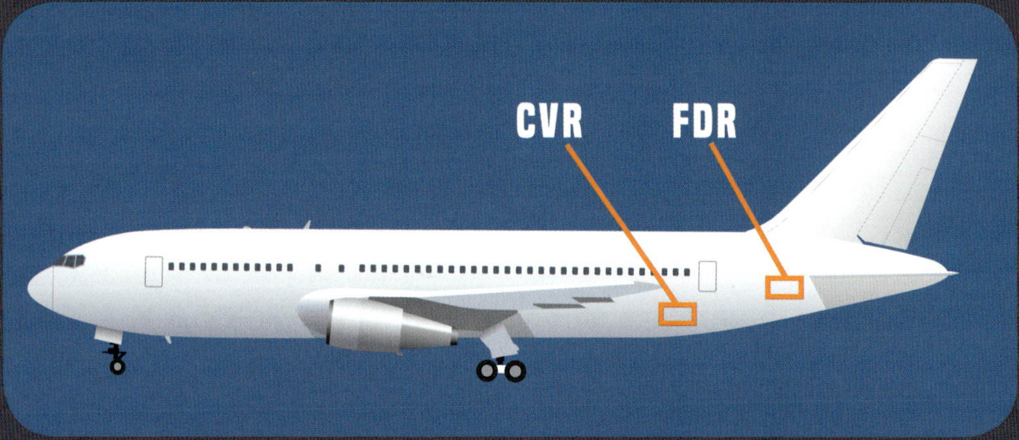

The CVR and FDR are placed toward the rear of an Airbus A330, where they are more likely to survive a crash. In Flight 447's case, the aircraft's tail section was the largest piece of debris recovered, meaning the rear survived better than the rest of the aircraft. Why do you think the tail area is more likely to survive a crash?

A WORSENING SITUATION

One guess as to why the crew pushed the nose up is that they thought the plane could not stall. With autopilot, there are systems designed to force a plane out of a stall. But once the autopilot switched off, these protections were gone.

Another pitot tube started working again. All of the airplane's systems were now operating normally.

But the plane's nose was still up even though the aircraft was falling out of the sky. The engines were at maximum thrust.

Both Bonin and Robert were at the controls. Both seats had a control stick. But only one pilot is designed to fly the aircraft at a time. While Bonin was pulling back to command a climb, Robert was pushing forward to command a descent. The plane just continued to drop with the nose pointing up.

ON AUTOPILOT

In the old days, pilots performed all flight tasks manually. They decided on the flight's route. They selected altitude, speed, and direction. They used the stick, rudder pedals, and throttle levers to adjust parts of the plane such as the engine to fly the planned route. Performing all these tasks on a long flight can be mentally tiring. In the modern airliner, the Flight Management System determines the best route with altitudes and speeds. Then the autopilot automatically adjusts parts of the plane to keep the plane on the route. The pilots check the route and monitor the plane's path while performing all the pilot duties.

PERSPECTIVES

STRANGE BEHAVIOR

Once Flight 447's black boxes were discovered, people had questions. For airline pilot and flight instructor Chris Nutter, there was simply no reasonable explanation for the copilots' actions. "If [Bonin is flying] straight and level and he's got no airspeed, I don't know why he'd pull back," Nutter said. He added that the proper thing to do would be to check the other instruments before making a decision. "Apparently that didn't happen [in this case]," he said.

THE CAPTAIN RETURNS

Finally, Dubois came back into the cockpit. It was a confusing situation. At this point, the aircraft was falling at 10,000 feet (3,048 m) per minute.

The crew finally realized they were falling and not climbing. Robert grabbed the stick and pushed it forward. This would help the plane to nose down and pick up speed, ending the stall. Robert pleaded out loud for the plane to climb.

Bonin replied, "But I've had the stick back the whole time."

In that moment, the problem became clear to Robert and Dubois. Dubois immediately told Bonin not to climb. But at this point, the aircraft was 2,000 feet (610 m) above the water. There was no time to descend to pick up speed and recover from the stall.

"We're going to crash," Robert said. "This can't be happening!" Seconds later, the CVR stopped.

FURTHER EVIDENCE

Chapter Four discusses what investigators learned from the black boxes. Identify the main point of this chapter, as well as supporting evidence. Then go to the website below and find a quote to support that point. Does the quote support evidence already in the chapter, or does it provide new evidence?

THE TRAGIC CRASH OF FLIGHT AF447 SHOWS THE UNLIKELY BUT CATASTROPHIC CONSEQUENCES OF AUTOMATION

abdocorelibrary.com/air-france-flight-447

CHAPTER FIVE

THE AFTERMATH

The investigation concluded that faulty airspeed readings, combined with pilot error, were the ultimate causes of the crash. The investigators' final report called for several changes to ensure that such an accident never happened again.

Some were already underway, such as the replacement of pitot tubes. But the nonmechanical causes of the crash could not be fixed so easily. Pilots needed more training on how to handle situations like Flight 447. Specifically, pilots needed more training on flying manually with conflicting air speeds.

Automation had taken over a lot of the airline industry. With so many planes in the

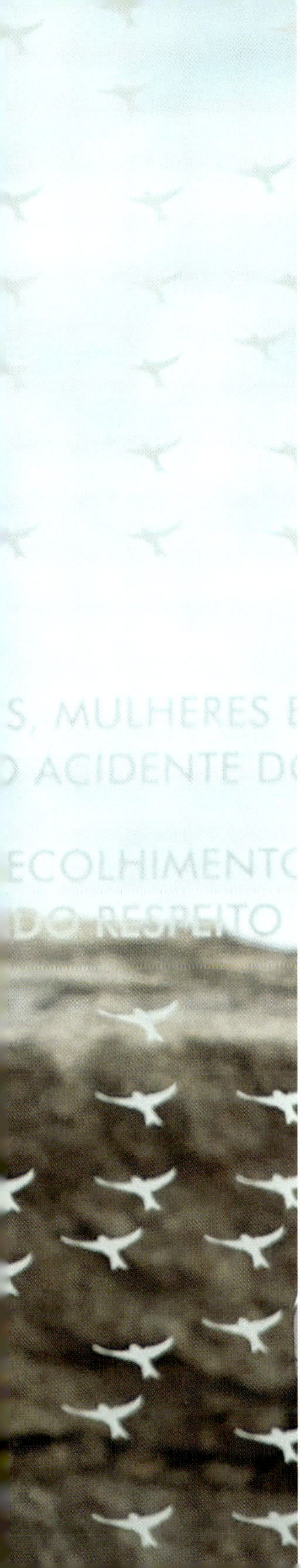

A relative of Flight 447 victims studies a memorial to those victims.

SIMILAR INCIDENT

In December 2014, AirAsia Flight 8501 was flying from Surabaya, Indonesia, to Singapore. After entering a storm, the plane dropped off radar minutes later. A computer malfunction commanded the plane to rock left and right and then climb into a stall. It crashed into the Java Sea. All 162 people on board died. While the broken rudder was the cause of the crash, pilot error was also to blame. The crew failed to recognize the problem until it was too late.

air, autopilot could fly routes more precisely and avoid human error. Pilots had so much to learn that they received very little training on flying manually at high altitudes. After Flight 447, pilots were required to practice getting out of a stall.

Instrumentation could also be improved. Planes have a sensor to tell pilots when they are in danger of a stall. This is known as an "angle of attack" indicator. The report recommended adding a display in the cockpit as a back-up. But this indicator was never added. Pilots were trained to use other data to

It is important that pilots receive training for many possible situations before they fly.

determine stall conditions. Opponents of the indicator argued pilots wouldn't use it.

EASIER SAID THAN DONE?

Some changes took a long time to make. Another recommendation was to require pilots to report the aircraft position regularly. It wasn't until another jet disappeared in 2014, Malaysian Airlines Flight 370, that a standard for reporting was set. Planes now signal their location every 15 minutes.

People again became interested in the idea to add an angle of attack indicator display in 2019. There also was a larger ongoing debate about automation.

PERSPECTIVES

AIR FRANCE RESPONSE

Flight 447 dealt a huge blow to Air France. It was the airline's second high-profile crash in ten years. In 2000, the supersonic Concorde airliner had crashed just after takeoff in Paris. Pilot error was found to be partially to blame for the crash of Flight 447. It was a major embarrassment. Air France blamed the confusing environment of the cockpit. The company insisted its pilots had been properly trained. "In this deteriorated aircraft cockpit environment, the crew, with the skills of one flight captain and two first officers, were committed to carrying out their task of piloting the aircraft to the very end," stated part of Air France's official response to the crash.

How much is too much? Should pilots be required to fly manually more often?

The crash of Air France Flight 447 should never have happened. It took a tragedy to reveal a problem nobody knew existed. Fortunately, in the decade since, the exact problem has not happened again. But pilots had to remain vigilant and rely on their training to keep it that way.

STRAIGHT TO THE SOURCE

Pilot Chelsey Sullenberger is famous for making an emergency landing in 2009 on the Hudson River in New York. All passengers survived. In 2019, he said of the state of flight automation:

> *It is not easier or cheaper or requires less training to fly an automated airplane. It frequently requires more, because you have to have a deep understanding of how a system works, including the dark corners, the counterintuitive things it might do in certain circumstances. Many foreign carriers are trying to take people with zero flying experience, put them in simulators and quickly put them in the right seat of a jetliner. They don't have the experience, knowledge, skills and confidence to be the absolute master of the aircraft start to finish.*

Source: Ralph Vartabedian and Samantha Masunaga. "Lion Air Crash Shows Cockpit Computers Are No Substitute for Pilot Skills." *Los Angeles Times*. Los Angeles Times, February 4, 2019. Web. July 18, 2019.

Changing Minds

Take a position on whether or not automated flight is a good thing. Then imagine that your best friend has the opposite opinion. Write a short essay trying to change your friend's mind. Include facts and details that support your reasons.

FAST FACTS

- Air France Flight 447 was a normally scheduled passenger flight from Rio de Janeiro, Brazil, to Paris, France, on May 31, 2009.
- The flight vanished from radar in the early morning hours of June 1, 2009.
- After the plane failed to contact the next air traffic control station, a search began in the Atlantic Ocean.
- After several weeks, the search turned up many pieces of debris, but no survivors nor the aircraft's black boxes.
- Two years later, the cockpit voice recorder and flight data recorder were recovered.
- With this data, investigators determined that a combination of failed equipment and pilot error caused the plane to stall and drop from the sky.
- Training for pilots was improved to prevent such errors from happening again.
- Some people have tried to add an angle of attack indicator display in cockpits, but others argue that is unnecessary.
- The debate continues as to how much automation is safe in aircraft.

www.voegol.com
PR-GXF
TOTAL
COMMITTED TO BETTER ENERGY

STOP AND THINK

Tell the Tale

Chapter Two describes the search for the wreckage of Flight 447. Imagine you were one of the people involved in the search. Write 200 words about what the journey would be like. What sort of things would you be looking for?

Surprise Me

Chapter Four describes the sequence of events that led to the crash of Flight 447. After reading this chapter, what two or three facts about airplanes did you find the most surprising? Write a few sentences about each fact. Why did you find each fact surprising?

Dig Deeper

After reading this book, what questions do you still have about Air France Flight 447? With an adult's help, find a few reliable resources that can help you answer your questions. Write a paragraph about what you learned.

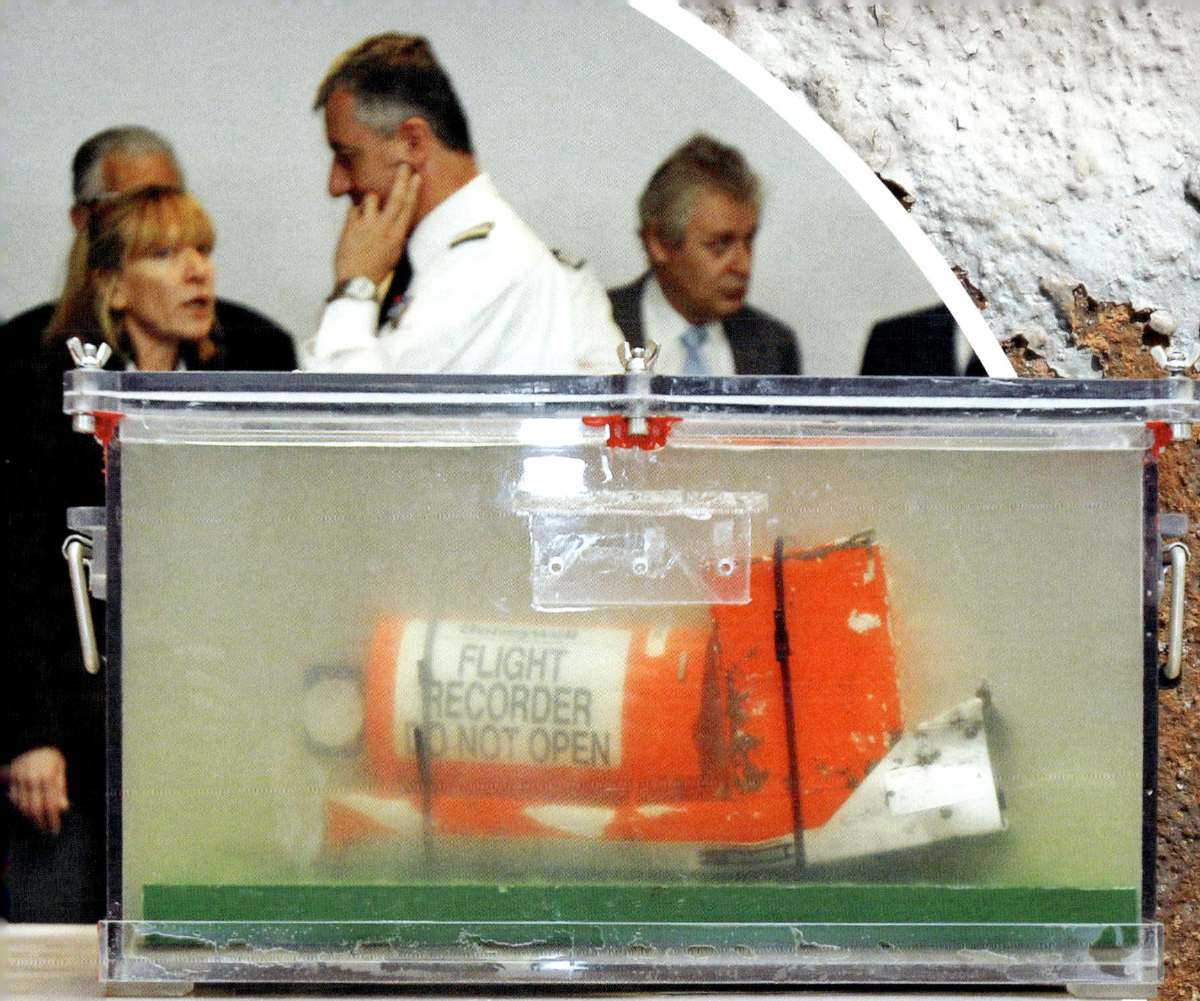

You Are There

This book discusses the effect of Flight 447 on future aviation. Imagine you are a pilot reading the report about what went wrong on Flight 447. Write a journal entry about ways to make sure you are prepared in an emergency situation. What mistakes would you want to avoid? Be sure to add plenty of detail to your notes.

GLOSSARY

airliner
a type of large airplane designed to carry passengers

altitude
how high up something is

autopilot
an automated system designed to fly an aircraft

cockpit
the place on an airplane where pilots fly it

copilot
a pilot who assists the captain in flying the plane

debris
broken pieces that come off of a larger object

radar
a method of tracking aircraft or other objects as they move

sensor
a device that detects something such as airspeed or temperature and reports the information to a person

stick
the main control input on an aircraft that directs it to turn or go up or down

thrust
the level of power at which airplane engines operate

turbulence
a patch of rough air that can cause an aircraft to bounce around in flight

ONLINE RESOURCES

To learn more about Air France Flight 447, visit our free resource websites below.

Core Library CONNECTION
FREE! COMMON CORE MULTIMEDIA RESOURCES

Visit **abdocorelibrary.com** or scan this QR code for free Common Core resources for teachers and students, including vetted activities, multimedia, and booklinks, for deeper subject comprehension.

Booklinks NONFICTION NETWORK
FREE! ONLINE NONFICTION RESOURCES

Visit **abdobooklinks.com** or scan this QR code for free additional online weblinks for further learning. These links are routinely monitored and updated to provide the most current information available.

LEARN MORE

The Big Book of Airplanes. New York: DK Publishing, 2016.

Hamilton, John. *Test Pilot*. Minneapolis, MN: Abdo Publishing, 2016.

INDEX

About the Author

Todd Kortemeier is a children's book author, sportswriter, and aviation enthusiast from Minneapolis.